my very first
Nativity Play

Words by **Lois Rock** ☆ Pictures by **Alex Ayliffe**

'Thanks for making the dress,' said Jennifer to her mother. 'It's just right for being Mary.'

The Christmas play was about to begin.

Suddenly, Jennifer didn't feel
as brave as before.

'Everyone chose you to be Mary,' said her
mother, 'because you've just had a new
baby brother.'

Jennifer – well, Mary – went on stage.
An angel appeared.

'Hello,' said the angel. 'God has chosen
you. You are to have a baby.'

'I'm not,' said Mary. After all,
she knew all about babies.

'God wants you to be
the mother of Jesus,'
said the angel.
'God's son.'

Mary shook her head slowly.
'That would be a miracle.'

'It will be,' said the angel.

'Joseph won't be pleased,'
said Mary.

'I'll tell him,' said
the angel.

Someone pulled back a curtain.
Joseph was asleep in a little bed.

'Hello,' said the angel.

Joseph sat up.

'God has chosen you to look after Mary,' said the angel.

'I know,' said Joseph. 'I'm going to marry her.'

'Mary is going to have a baby, Jesus,' said the angel. 'He is God's son. Please look after them both.'

'People will know the baby isn't mine,' said Joseph. 'They'll gossip.'

'People are like that,' agreed the angel.

Joseph went over to Mary.

'I promise to take care of you and the baby,' he said. 'Now we must go to Bethlehem. It's to do with the emperor. And taxes.'

Together they walked to Bethlehem.

They went to an inn.

'We need a room for the night,' said Joseph.

'Sorry,' said the innkeeper. 'No room.'

'I'm going to have a baby,' said Mary.

'When?' growled the innkeeper.

'Who knows?' said Mary. 'Babies come when they come.'

'Oh dear,' said the innkeeper. 'I'll clean a bit of the stable for you.'

There was an ox and a donkey in the stable.

'Move up,' said the innkeeper.

'Moo,' said the ox.

'Ee-aaw,' said the donkey.

Mary and Joseph sat down on some straw.

'At least we're saving money,' said Joseph.

'We'll be spending more when we have the baby,' warned Mary.

'I know,' said Joseph glumly.

A curtain swung across the stage and it went dark.

When the lights came on, it was for the
next part of the play. All the shepherds
walked on stage.

They sat down.

Then the sheep walked on stage.

All of them.

A bright light shone as the angel appeared.

'Fear not,' said the angel.

'Pa-aardon,' said a sheep loudly. The whole flock giggled.

'Be afraid,' whispered the teacher. 'Be very afraid.'

'Fear not,' said the angel. 'I bring good news. God's son has been born in Bethlehem. He is Jesus, God's chosen king.

'He has come to welcome people into God's kingdom.'

More lights shone. There were more angels.

The music teacher played a little tune on the harp.

Then all the angels sang. It was a lovely song.

The shepherds listened politely.

The sheep were truly amazed.

Then it was dark again.

'Do you think we were dreaming?' asked
a shepherd.

'We can go to Bethlehem,' said another.

'If we find the baby Jesus, we will know.'

They set off, and the sheep followed.

Someone pulled back a curtain.

There was Mary and Joseph and the baby.

'What's the baby's name?' asked one
of the shepherds.

'Joshua,' said Joseph.

Mary gulped. That was her
baby brother's real name.

'It's Jesus,' said Mary.
'Like Joshua... only
different. It's a
Bible name.'

'So now we have found Jesus, and we believe what the angel told us,' said the shepherd.

The three wise men stood in front
of the big stage curtains. They looked lost.

'Do you know where we're going?' asked one.

'I'm not sure,' said the second.

'But we can still see the star,'
        said the third.

            'Let's keep going,' they said.

        They walked this way
        and that way.

            They arrived in front of a king.

'Your Majesty,' they said. 'We're looking for a newborn king.'

'A newborn king?' said the king. 'Not in my palace. My advisers might know.'

He walked over to someone who was holding a scroll.

'Do you know anything about a newborn king?' he asked.

'Yes,' said the adviser. 'It's written here. One day, God will send a special king. He will be born in Bethlehem.'

'Bother,' said the king crossly.

'Go to Bethlehem,' the king told the wise men. 'Then come back and tell me where to find the baby.'

The wise men went.

The star led the way.

The big curtains swung back.

The star went and stood right by
the place where Joseph and Mary
and the baby were.

'The baby king!' said a wise man.
'I am bringing him a gift of gold.'

'I bring frankincense,'
said the second.

'I bring myrrh,'
said the third.

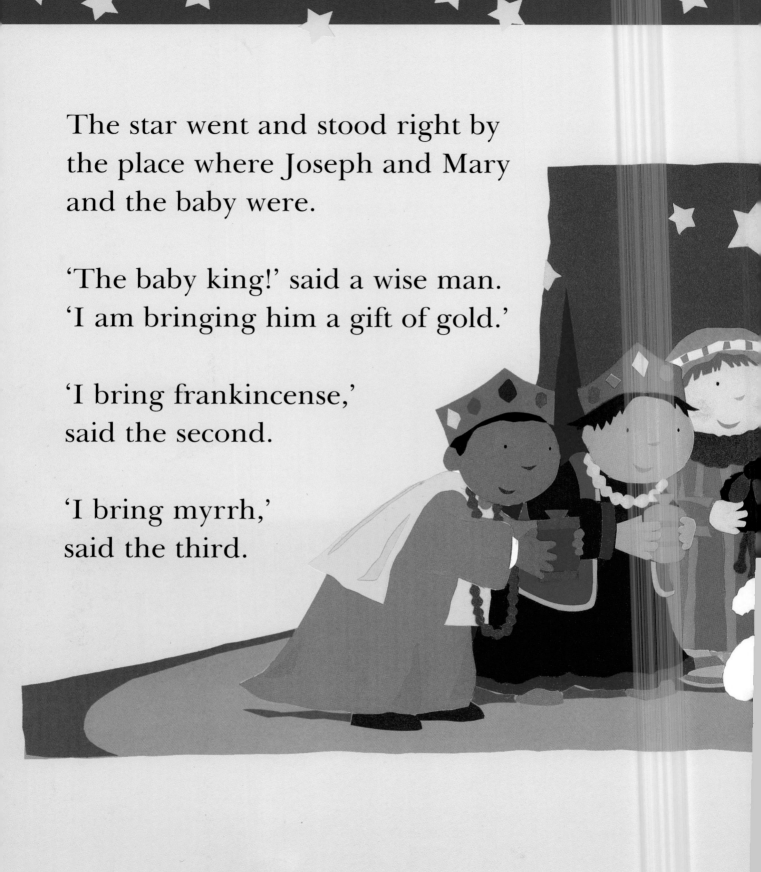

Everyone sang a carol.

Jennifer carried her baby brother back to his cradle.

She had a question she hardly dared to ask.

'Was the play good?' she asked her mother as they walked home. 'Did you think you were really in Bethlehem?'

'Oh yes,' said her mother. 'And more than that, I thought that I could see all the way to heaven.'

The stars shone even more
brightly in the night sky.

For Abi A.A

Text by Lois Rock
Illustrations copyright © 2005 Alex Ayliffe
This edition copyright © 2005 Lion Hudson

The moral rights of the author and illustrator
have been asserted

A Lion Children's Book
an imprint of
Lion Hudson plc
Mayfield House, 256 Banbury Road,
Oxford OX2 7DH, England
www.lionhudson.com
ISBN 0 7459 4978 9

First edition 2005
10 9 8 7 6 5 4 3 2 1 0

A catalogue record for this book is available
from the British Library

Typeset in 22/30 Baskerville BT
Printed and bound in Singapore